Neighbourhood regeneration

Resourcing community involvement

Pete Duncan and Sally Thomas

UMᵖ　　　　　　　AN

The POLICY
P~P
PRESS

First published in Great Britain in March 2000 by

The Policy Press
34 Tyndall's Park Road
Bristol BS8 1PY
UK

Tel no   +44 (0)117 954 6800
Fax no   +44 (0)117 973 7308
E-mail   tpp@bristol.ac.uk
http://www.bristol.ac.uk/Publications/TPP

© The Policy Press and the Joseph Rowntree Foundation 2000

Published for the Joseph Rowntree Foundation by The Policy Press

ISBN 1 86134 227 6

Pete Duncan and **Sally Thomas** are Partners in Social Regeneration Consultants. Social Regeneration Consultants is based in North East England. It specialises in community-based urban regeneration, working closely with local communities on a broad range of initiatives.

The **Joseph Rowntree Foundation** has supported this project as part of its programme of research and innovative development projects, which it hopes will be of value to policy makers, practitioners and service users. The facts presented and views expressed in this report are, however, those of the authors and not necessarily those of the Foundation.

Cover design by Qube Design Associates, Bristol.
Front cover, top centre photograph of The Firthmoor Community Partnership Board, Darlington, County Durham, kindly supplied by Pete Duncan.
Printed in Great Britain by Hobbs the Printers Ltd, Southampton

Contents

Acknowledgements

We would like to thank the many organisations and individuals who helped with the research for this study. In particular we would like to thank the following for their detailed comments on the initial draft:

Mary Doyle	Development Trusts Association
Stephen Dunmore	New Opportunities Fund
Clive Dutton	Sandwell Metropolitan Borough Council
Vandna Gohill	National Lottery Charities Board
Adrian Moran	Housing Corporation
John Routledge	Urban Forum
Marilyn Taylor	O-Regen
Alison West	Community Development Foundation
Charles Wood	Community Matters

We would also like to record our thanks to John Low at the Joseph Rowntree Foundation for his ongoing support for this project. A full list of those consulted is included in the Appendix.

Most of all, we would like to pay tribute to the many communities we have worked with and who have helped us to develop our knowledge and understanding of the important issues which underlie this study.

Introduction

The role of local communities in neighbourhood-based regeneration programmes is firmly in the political and policy spotlight. Research over the past six years – much of it carried out by the Joseph Rowntree Foundation (JRF) – has demonstrated that community involvement is a crucial prerequisite for sustainability. Communities cannot involve themselves fully in these programmes unless they have the capacity to do so, and many do not. They usually need help and support to equip them with the knowledge, skills and understanding to put them on at least an equal basis with professionals – they need to build their capacity. All this is now widely accepted by both government and practitioners and forms the basis for a number of recent initiatives, such as New Deal for Communities, Sure Start and Health Action Zones.

However, the stakeholders in many deprived neighbourhoods, and not least communities themselves, remain uncertain about how best to deliver this agenda in practical terms. There remains a wide gap between the policy rhetoric and the reality on the ground. Improving community access to the resources they need to be able to deliver their part of the new agenda is clearly a central issue.

Existing resources for capacity building deprived communities are not insubstantial, although they are increasingly being targeted on a limited number of priority areas. Even here, such resources are not always well coordinated. Their potential impact on tackling deprivation through encouraging community self-help is not always well understood. Although we have become reasonably adept at evaluating the hard outputs from regeneration programmes, we remain much less confident when dealing with the softer outcomes. Assessing the impact of resourcing community capacity building comes firmly into this category.

Communities in priority deprived neighbourhoods are faced with an often bewildering array of potential sources of support, all with their own criteria and restrictions. Communities with urgent needs, but who are unlucky enough to live in non-priority areas, are faced with few, if any, potential sources of support. The largely informal networks rely exclusively on volunteers, but since we know that volunteering in deprived areas is much less common than elsewhere, the potential of these networks to bring cohesion and stability to communities is inevitably limited.

The real challenge is to find ways of resourcing the development of these informal networks which lead to broader and deeper community activity, offering the prospect of self-sustaining communities in the long term. There is also an absence of coordination between funding agencies which is compounded by a range of other factors which tend to inhibit, rather than promote, grass-roots community activity.

Methodology

This study set out to examine all these issues and to point a way forward. Its primary aim was to undertake a review of the current resources available for community capacity building within area regeneration programmes and consider where changes are needed. It was confined to a consideration of urban areas.

We have framed our deliberations within the context of the government's emerging national strategy for neighbourhood renewal, *Bringing Britain together* (SEU, 1998). We were keen to establish what works and what does not, how existing funding streams might be improved, what additional resources might be needed to fill the gaps in current provision, who should provide them and how they might best be targeted. We particularly wanted to establish an effective link between the resourcing of community involvement and emerging proposals for neighbourhood management and joined-up action by regeneration agencies.

Our methodology included structured interviews with a wide range of national organisations and a limited questionnaire survey of local agencies involved in area regeneration programmes. This enabled us to create a useful picture of current practice and to assemble a broad cross-section of views and opinions from those with extensive experience in this field on the best way forward for community involvement.

Perhaps most importantly, the report draws on our extensive experience of working directly with local communities involved in regeneration initiatives throughout the country.

Some definitions

Community capacity building

There is much current discussion about the need for capacity building work with communities. During the course of this study it became obvious that people use this term in different ways to describe different things. The following definition may be helpful:

> **Community capacity building** involves development work which strengthens the ability of community-based organisations and groups to build their structures, systems, people and skills. This enables them to better define and achieve their objectives and engage in consultation, planning, development and management. It also helps them to take an active and equal role in partnerships with other organisations and agencies. Capacity building includes aspects of training, consultancy, organisational and

personal development, mentoring and peer group support, organised in a planned manner and based on the principles of empowerment and equality. (adapted from Skinner, 1997)

There is, consequently, an important difference between capacity building individuals and capacity building communities as groups, although, in many cases, the former may contribute substantially to the latter.

To illustrate the point, providing the finance for a group of trainees to undertake a GNVQ course in construction skills would qualify as community capacity building only if the primary intention was to establish a community-based maintenance squad or business. If, however, the primary intention was simply to increase the skills and job prospects for the trainees as individuals, it would not.

Social capital

The term 'social capital' is also increasingly used in the context of community-based regeneration. There is even less clarity and understanding of what this means. We have adopted the following definition:

> **Social capital** is the intangible web of relationships and widespread participation in communities and community organisations that holds them together. It is essentially goodwill, sympathy, empathy and neighbourliness among the individuals and households who make up social units. These may be communities defined by geography and/or interest. Social capital can be created, extended and maintained by such activities as street parties, community picnics, community arts activities, carnivals and a variety of other community gatherings. (adapted from Knight et al, 1998)

Social capital, engendered as it is by a wide range of community organisations, including tenants' associations, schools, churches and pubs, is therefore the social 'glue' which makes local communities work – the informal networks which are often invisible to outsiders, but which are such a vital component of community life.

The policy context

Government policy on neighbourhood regeneration

During the last 10 years, successive governments have placed an increasing emphasis on regeneration programmes which are carefully targeted, successfully integrate resources and delivery agencies, build effective partnerships, and fully involve local communities affected by the programmes. These are all laudable objectives. Many lessons have been learned and these have helped to re-shape successive regeneration programmes. There have been concerted attempts at national, regional and local levels to achieve substantive and sustainable regeneration in some of the most deprived communities in the UK.

However, there is still a long way to go. There is much to be said for the general concept of targeting regeneration resources on defined neighbourhoods, preferably within a comprehensive city- or district-wide regeneration strategy. But the way in which this concept has been applied has been one of the fundamental reasons for the continuing

> ... failure to get to grips with the problems of the poorest neighbourhoods ... [where] public money has been wasted on programmes that were never going to work and generations of people living in poor neighbourhoods have grown up with the odds stacked against them. (SEU, 1998, Summary, section 8)

Competition for area regeneration resources

From City Challenge through to the Single Regeneration Budget (SRB), the structural

approach has been the same. Area regeneration programmes are predicated upon a premise which seeks to address fundamental social and economic problems through a largely competitive process in which bids are made, in the main, by local authorities in accordance with their priorities. Large sums of money are then allocated to areas of often acute poverty and extreme need. These areas are defined not by residents, but according to national indicators of need such as the Department of the Environment, Transport and the Regions' Local Index of Deprivation (DETR, 1998a). The money has to be spent quickly, in accordance with the timetables and priorities of local and central government. The resources and responsibility are handed over to institutions which are still in the main concerned with retaining power rather than sharing it and tackling what they consider needs to be done from their own perspective.

In short, area regeneration programmes have, for the most part, been *imposed* upon communities who have then become *recipients* of activity rather than active, equal partners in their own futures. It is not a recipe for long-term success. It is becoming increasingly obvious that until trust, responsibility and decision making are vested in local people themselves, regeneration programmes will continue to achieve, at best, only partial success. This key message has now been recognised in the arrangements for the New Deal for Communities programme.

The need for preventative action

Urban regeneration policy has traditionally taken a reactive approach to area-based problems. But there is much to be said for balancing this with preventative action. Recent research (see Burrows and Rhodes, 1998) shows that current targeting of the 'worst estates' as perceived by local authorities and measured against standard statistical indices of need, misses a significant proportion of residents living in what they themselves perceive to be squalid neighbourhoods. If these residents are denied access to programmes and resources which enable them to address their local conditions, their neighbourhoods will quickly become tomorrow's problems. While 20% of the fifth round of the SRB can, in theory, be used for such neighbourhoods, this is insufficient to meet current needs. More importantly, in the context of this study, the bidding process and requirements militate against such communities accessing the funding themselves.

There may well be a case for mini-regeneration programmes which specifically support a limited number of projects based around self-help. In some situations, such limited programmes may in themselves be sufficient to arrest the deterioration of declining neighbourhoods. Where this is not possible, they could be implemented as a precursor to larger-scale programmes. This would enable communities to identify the problems, start to take practical steps to address some of them, establish consultative and participatory structures, develop partnerships with agencies and draw up a comprehensive community plan. This would form the basis of a bid to the main programmes. It is an approach which has obvious implications for resourcing community capacity building.

A community-led focus

Whether reactive or preventative, small scale or large, there is now a widely held view that area regeneration must be looked at in a much more community-focused way:

- proposals should be developed, wherever possible, by communities themselves;
- they should be encouraged to take the lead, involving local authorities, statutory agencies and other stakeholders in community-led partnerships;
- these will inevitably take longer to develop and carry a higher risk so communities will require the financial and technical resources to support and manage the process;

- mainstream policies and programmes will have to acquire much more flexibility, 'bending' to meet local circumstances;
- implementation will require a 10-year timescale within which to achieve results;
- national and local political support and financial resources will have to be guaranteed for this 10-year period.

It is a significant challenge and one which many communities could rise to, but it would be a mistake to conclude that all communities will inevitably want to take the lead in the regeneration of their neighbourhoods. Many will be content to enter partnerships with local authorities and others, to share responsibility for implementation. Although it is certainly right to encourage local communities to play a more significant role in neighbourhood regeneration than many have done in the past, progress is often likely to be incremental and highly dependent on local circumstances.

It is important, therefore, to be realistic about what can be achieved, although realism must not be used as an excuse for inactivity. Enabling communities to take on the level of involvement they would like in their neighbourhoods is a significant challenge, and will require not only new resources, but also major and lasting change in the culture and operation of many regeneration agencies. If community-led regeneration is to be effective on a significant scale, the structural approach upon which area or neighbourhood programmes are currently predicated will need to be reviewed.

National, regional and local structures

The problems associated with the current approach to area regeneration have an impact at national, regional and local levels. It is clear from our research that they create often insuperable problems for communities.

Nationally, despite recent and welcome moves to promote 'joined-up thinking' and greater policy coordination, the rigidity of government departmentalism continues to create fragmented policies and funding at a local level. There is an ever-increasing and often confusing array of government initiatives, each reflecting different aspects of national policy objectives. Their application through regeneration programmes often takes little account of local variations and involves high costs in time and resources for local organisations and their staff. The political imperatives of all governments – to do things that are new and do them quickly – is not always helpful.

Regional coordination

Regionally, the Government Offices represent some of the key government departments and were expected to deliver a more integrated approach. There are, however, key departments missing. There are too few civil servants located in the Government Offices who have the expertise and/or capacity to advise and support community-led programmes. Their monitoring and evaluating role is insufficiently supported by effective sanctions to enable them, when necessary, to persuade local authorities to pursue a more inclusive, community-based approach. Their local and regional knowledge is not always used to best effect by central government when developing policy.

The new Regional Development Agencies (RDAs) present a further cause for concern. Another strata of regeneration management, separating the SRB from mainstream programmes, will necessitate additional consultative and coordination mechanisms. Despite a remit to act on both social exclusion and sustainable development, it is questionable to what extent all the RDAs will recognise the need to take on a social as well as an economic regeneration role – some are beginning to do so, but others may be more reluctant. There is likely to be a close correlation between the level of community-based regeneration activity in a region and the willingness of the RDA to take up a social regeneration brief. RDAs with lower levels of community activity in their regions may be less enthusiastic about going strongly down this route. Even where they do, local communities will need time to understand and engage with them.

Local commitment to community regeneration

Locally, where it really counts, the problems evident at national and regional levels accumulate with others. Local authority cultures and structures tend to replicate the departmentalism and political imperatives of

central government. Because the majority of area regeneration programmes are local authority-led and managed, these institutional structures and approaches are further replicated in the relationship between the authority and local communities. Partnership Boards, both in composition and culture, often mimic council committees.

There is, of course, a wide variation between and within local authorities in their commitment to community involvement. Although real progress has been made in some areas, too many councils have paid lip service to it in order to secure regeneration resources – addressing the issue in a tokenistic way when they have done so. Even where there is a strong commitment to involving the community, there is often little understanding of how to achieve it. Poorly thought-out attempts to implement often dramatic change through a combination of agencies, services and resources on a defined area can exacerbate, rather than resolve, many community tensions, particularly those of race and gender.

The impact on communities

Research for this study indicates that communities themselves are bearing the brunt of these unresolved problems. At a local level, the array of programmes resulting from national policy is now bewildering. Some communities are suffering consultation and research fatigue. Consultation is often viewed by residents as being too little, too late and having little, if any, visible impact on the programmes. Action research is often viewed as a way for agencies to show that they are doing something.

Timescales are dictated by national, regional and local programmes and are invariably too short for communities to work to. There are rarely any 'rules of engagement' which establish clear parameters, roles and responsibilities: What are the aims and objectives? Who is involved? What status do they have? Are there rights of veto? There is little clarity in the institutional roles and responsibilities at local, regional and national levels and the accountability relationships between them. Many of these problems are now being addressed through the New Deal for Communities programme and the Local Government Association's New Commitment to

Regeneration, but it will take time for this to spread to other neighbourhood regeneration initiatives.

Unequal partnerships

Partnerships, for all their intrinsic merit, are not equal. Invariably councillors, officers and professionals dominate boards and chair meetings. There are partnerships in name, but only rarely in practice. While the situation is improving, there is still too little emphasis on capacity building, particularly prior to and during bid preparation. Many communities do not have access to 'honest brokers', independent intermediary organisations, for support and advice.

Community development workers are often the main link a community has with programmes, funding and decision-making structures, but they are in increasingly short supply. Those that remain are often compromised by being employees of the agencies leading the programmes, usually local authorities. They rarely have enough status, senior management backing or access to infrastructure support, such as funding, financial advice and administrative assistance.

Accessing the funding

There is not enough access to funding for communities to carry out their own initiatives. Small-scale funding for resident-led consultation, the hire of a mini-bus, the cost of a crèche or a social event to bring the community together is woefully lacking, and mainstream funding sources rarely accommodate such needs. Residents and community development workers often find themselves having to spend time and effort fundraising for these small but essential activities.

Finally, there is never enough time to establish the basis of meaningful, ongoing community involvement. What takes years, many agencies try to do in months, sometimes even weeks. Short-term capacity is created, only to be replaced by long-term incapacity.

Ultimately, the issue is one of power and control, too much of which is still in the hands of local authorities, statutory agencies and professionals. This has resulted in the

"domination of complex inter-agency regeneration initiatives by professionals with little transparency or accountability to their local communities" (Hall and Mawson, 1999, p v).

Focusing on outcomes

It has also resulted in the elevation of product over process; based on the assumption that the product, be it new housing, a refurbished community centre or a locally-based training centre, is really what regeneration is about. The process has not yet been accepted for what it is – the key determinant in whether the products will be appropriate and sustainable. The emphasis in regeneration programmes on tangible outputs has further exacerbated this distortion. While there is a growing acceptance of the validity of less tangible measures, or outcomes, for assessing the success of programmes, further research and thought needs to be given to how best this could be achieved.

In reality, we have not yet moved far enough from the 1980s' approach to urban regeneration, which emphasised physical renewal over the developmental process of empowering local people to achieve real and lasting benefits for themselves and their communities. While there is widespread agreement that this approach failed to engage a vital resource in area regeneration – local residents – the necessary conditions to redress the balance have yet to be either fully understood or implemented.

What is acknowledged is that local communities need a range of support mechanisms and financial resources if they are to be able to become involved in area regeneration on any sort of equal basis. This approach has come to be embodied by the term capacity building. The next chapter looks at how this approach developed and what is really meant by capacity building. It considers the current problems preventing capacity building being applied to maximum benefit in the communities affected by and involved in area regeneration programmes.

The importance of community capacity building

The City Challenge programmes of the early 1990s required community involvement in area regeneration as a key aspect of programme development and delivery. Previously, during the regeneration programmes of the 1980s, the requirements to achieve economic and physical regeneration were at the forefront of government policy. While a handful of the agencies delivering regeneration during this period, in particular some of the urban development corporations, chose to incorporate social programmes into their work, they were not required to do so. It was a serious mistake. Subsequent evaluation of the impact of policy during this period highlighted evidence of increased social polarisation within many of our cities.

This resulted in local communities, and local authorities, being accorded a more substantial role in the development and delivery of programmes. It was acknowledged that they should be involved. What this meant in practice and how it would be achieved was open to wide interpretation as there was little guidance. Some City Challenge programmes achieved a high level of community involvement; others very little. But the experience of all contributed towards a more sophisticated appreciation and understanding of the need for community involvement along with greater knowledge of how it might be achieved.

With the advent of the SRB, principles had developed for involving communities in regeneration. These included communities influencing and participating in decision making, managing regeneration projects and sustaining the regeneration process beyond the life of the initiative. But the key lesson that had been learned was that the majority of communities

could not be involved in an equal and effective way unless intensive development work was done to build their strength. Capacity building was the key to success.

The Holy Grail of regeneration

Community capacity building is now at the forefront of many regeneration programmes – it has become the new Holy Grail. Round 5 of the government's SRB programme contains more than 3,000 separate capacity building initiatives. There will inevitably continue to be suspicion in some quarters that bidders may be using the right language, without necessarily having the understanding of, or commitment to, what lies behind it. Nevertheless, there is little doubt that the message is at least starting to get through.

It is now recognised that capacity building is central to achieving sustainable changes that will have a lasting impact, although what this means in practice is less clear. There is a danger that regeneration programmes will develop and institute a range of capacity building projects in an ad hoc and unstrategic way. This may reduce their individual and combined impact on the area, lead to disenchantment among communities and waste valuable social and financial resources.

Towards a pluralistic and flexible approach

Capacity building requires a pluralistic and flexible approach. It needs to be applied in different ways in different places according to existing levels of capacity and local circumstances. What it means and how it will be achieved in each area should be defined as part of every regeneration programme strategy. Overall aims and objectives need to be set, which can then be reviewed and measured, in the form of a capacity building plan. This should be an element of the overall delivery plan. Capacity building activities can then be prioritised and budgeted for over the lifetime of the programme. Capacity building should encompass a diverse range of approaches and projects. They may include training, education, mentoring, personal development, organisational development and consultancy work. In many neighbourhoods there will also be a need for a capacity building strategy to specifically address gender and disability issues and the needs of the black and minority ethnic community.

The type of capacity building that a community needs must be defined and prioritised by the community itself, if necessary with advice and support. This should be done prior to the bid documentation being put together. Capacity building involves risk. Some measures will work, others will not. It will be impossible to know beforehand which will succeed and which will fail, but it should be remembered that as much can be learned from the failures as from the successes.

The resourcing of capacity building clearly plays a vital role in the extent to which these general objectives are achieved. Currently, communities themselves have limited access to funding for capacity building. The major sources of potential funding are problematic:

- a disproportionate number are controlled by local authorities;
- it is difficult to access small amounts of funding, ie under £500;
- overly detailed and complex application forms are the norm;
- many require the (relatively costly) assistance of a consultant to complete;
- there can be a considerable delay between application and response;
- many sources are not widely known about.

In other words, there are few sources which are flexible, independent, quick and appropriate.

Capacity building other stakeholders

Now, as we move further from simply involving communities in regeneration towards encouraging communities to play an equal or lead role in regeneration programmes, capacity building becomes more critical. It becomes critical at more levels than simply local communities. In fact, building the capacity of communities to fully engage in area regeneration is but one element in the equation. The capacity of the voluntary sector has to be further developed and strengthened so it can fully support and advise communities. The capacity of local authorities, government departments and other agencies to integrate a community-based approach into their cultures in order to understand and actively work with communities and to their agenda must also be significantly increased.

Building the capacity of the private sector is also important. Companies and larger businesses are becoming increasingly involved in regeneration programmes, but more could be achieved, either directly or through charitable trusts and foundations, if the capacity of the private sector to understand their potential role in deprived communities was developed.

In conclusion, community capacity building is now accepted as an essential feature of successful, sustainable regeneration. There are problems with developing appropriate projects, implementation and, of course, resourcing. Some agencies see it simply as the latest hoop to jump through in order to access regeneration funding. But essentially the argument has been won.

The most significant impact of community capacity building, however, is yet to fully emerge. The logical long-term aim must be for many communities to become sufficiently strengthened to be able to lead neighbourhood regeneration programmes. In so doing, the balance of power will then start to shift away from local authorities and agencies in favour of communities. But for most regeneration programmes this is still some way off. In the short and medium term, equal involvement in regeneration partnerships may be as far as most communities wish to go. Encouraging those that want to go further should then become a priority and we may then start to see the community-based approach to area regeneration which is so often debated, but only rarely delivered.

Delivering a community-based approach to neighbourhood regeneration

A community-based approach to neighbourhood regeneration requires certain fundamental changes to current practices and policies. It also requires the introduction of new ones. From the research already done by JRF, we know much of what needs to happen (JRF, 1998, 1999).

Enabling communities to take the lead, be at the heart of the decision-making process and materially benefit from investment through jobs and community ownership of assets, is the foundation. This requires a range of capacity building initiatives, viewed as an integral part of the regeneration programme. These should include:

- the development of community visions and action plans;
- resourcing and supporting community involvement in partnerships;
- developing the strength of community organisations with the aim of managing and/or owning the projects and assets created by the programme;
- developing an infrastructure to support community organisations in the longer term;
- monitoring and evaluating progress, including the recording and dissemination of good practice.

It is clear from the research carried out for this study that many regeneration programmes now understand these necessities. In particular, they are implementing a wide range of capacity building projects. Some are making real efforts to shift the balance of power.

New capacity building measures

We need to go further, to extend capacity building to its logical conclusion. There are a number of newer capacity building measures that could and should be implemented in order to achieve a community-based approach to area regeneration. Some will depend on local circumstances, others are, arguably, essential features of any capacity building programme. All are aimed at shifting the balance of power in area regeneration programmes away from professionals and agencies towards residents. These measures include:

- Negotiating and agreeing a written contract or concord between the community and the agencies involved in the partnership. This would set out the nature of the relationships, roles and responsibilities involved, and would be regularly reviewed.
- Ensuring that community representatives chair and have the majority of places on Partnership Boards and other forums established as part of the programme.
- Encouraging and supporting consultation which is community-led. This would include street meetings, door-to-door surveys, audits and mapping, design days, walkabouts to identify problems, and community planning events. It would require training to provide residents with the necessary skills, funding to support the activities and, where appropriate, payment for residents.
- Supporting capacity building measures which are identified by the community. These will rarely fit into any conventional education or training parameters, but their relevance and appropriateness to the community should be the determining factor.

- Training for officers and professionals by the community – all too often it is assumed that only local people need training. Just as important is training for local authority officers and professionals from other agencies on community issues and community-based approaches. Such training should ideally be carried out by residents themselves.
- Organising visits to other projects and communities to see examples of good practice, discuss problems and encourage networking.
- More and better community-generated publicity and promotion, both to the wider world (the region and the country) and, perhaps more importantly, to local senior officers and members who are often not closely involved in programmes.
- Community groups with common interests coming together as consortia to create one voice, act collectively and pool expertise and funds.
- Locating local authority officers and agency professionals in communities. The importance of involving local people in regeneration programmes derives mainly from the fact that they experience the problems everyday and know better than most what is needed to put things right. The majority of professionals involved in area regeneration programmes might never live in the communities they are working with, but more could work in them.
- Support, where appropriate, for community entrepreneurs or champions, to pump-prime the capacity-building process and facilitate an equal place for communities at the regeneration table.

The importance of community development

Because of the unique relationship they have with communities, community development workers are, potentially, a vital resource for the professional agencies involved in neighbourhood regeneration. Unfortunately it is a potential which is only occasionally realised. The majority of agencies use community development staff as a warning bell for problems and a conduit for community engagement in their programmes and plans. All too rarely is community development understood and applied in a strategic way as a fundamental element in a multi-disciplinary approach to the improvement of deprived neighbourhoods. If used properly, the knowledge and expertise of community development workers can successfully identify priorities, target resources more effectively, and improve relationships between residents and professionals.

The majority of community development workers are employed by local authorities. It is clear from our research that theirs is an important role in the development and delivery of neighbourhood regeneration programmes, as well as the delivery of local authority services and other functions. It also creates tensions. The agendas of local authorities can be at odds with the views and needs of communities and community development workers are often stuck in the middle. In some extreme cases, they can be used to manipulate communities. Participatory forums established by local authorities are all too often used to consult local opinion rather than genuinely move towards community or neighbourhood control of resources.

Some local authorities do not employ enough community development workers; others employ more, but their effectiveness suffers from a lack of strategic approach and status within the authority. In consequence, there is often an absence of clarity and respect externally about their roles and responsibilities. Community development is too often seen as a discretionary function and is vulnerable to cuts. Its long-term, non-output driven approach does not sit easily with the world of performance indicators and value for money. It is our perception as a result of the research for this study that the numbers of community development workers have declined steadily over the last 10 years, ironically the very same period over which significant sums of money have been invested in area regeneration programmes. Such sums, as we now know, represent a 'costly policy failure' having largely failed to stem ever widening social and economic division.

Reviewing the community development role

The role of community development and the actual and potential value it has in achieving neighbourhood regeneration needs to be reviewed and redefined. While such a comprehensive review is outside the scope of this study, we would advocate some clear practical steps that should be taken now in order to maximise the potential value of community development as the major resource for community involvement in neighbourhood regeneration. Community development posts should be extended within local authorities – there should be more of them – but the activity should be also be diversified, spreading it across a broader range of agencies and organisations. Finally, communities themselves should be encouraged and enabled to employ their own community development staff.

Local authorities should review their current approach to, and staffing of, community development. They need to develop a more strategic approach to it, both generally and within the context of neighbourhood regeneration. This implies consideration of the location, status, budgets and lines of accountability within the authority. It also necessitates capacity building within the authorities themselves, particularly of members and senior officers, in order to inculcate a community-based approach within those who have the access to resources and make the key decisions.

Some progress is being made in these areas, but more agencies involved in neighbourhood regeneration programmes should now be creating community development posts. Those involved in training and employment, housing, health and the arts in particular could be more proactive in this field. It would provide agencies with an important resource for meeting their aims and objectives in respect of community involvement and would also provide communities with a clear mechanism through which to engage with agencies which usually seem remote and inaccessible. It would diversify the community development base, and start to build a local infrastructure of community development workers which would maximise their impact in terms of capacity building, as well as providing peer support. The latter is particularly important for staff who are locally-based and subject to the continual pressures and tensions of working at a community level.

Putting local communities in the driving seat

There are two further critical factors in achieving community-led area regeneration which is sustainable in the longer term. The first is involving communities early; the second is enabling and empowering those communities that want to, to lead the succession strategy and take over the responsibility for long-term development and management.

It is clear from our research that only in the minority of programmes does either of these happen. The most common approach is that professionals prepare the bids and delivery plans at the outset and then the exit strategies at the end. The community gets involved in the middle. There are exceptions, such as Royds Community Association in Bradford. Here, a small group of local people, along with a local authority officer and a representative from the private sector, spent three years preparing detailed plans and proposals prior to submitting a major SRB bid. The success of the subsequent programme, particularly in the extent to which it is resident-led, is due in no small part to this thorough preparatory work which fully involved the community.

At the other end of the process, Waltham Forest Housing Action Trust has set up two community-based vehicles to ensure full community involvement in the future development of the area. The first is a community trust which will continue to implement a community and economic development strategy involving a range of capacity building projects. Importantly, in order to strengthen its financial base, it will have a borough-wide focus, with the ability to expand its workload and add value to other regeneration programmes in the area. In addition, a community-based housing association, run by a tenant-majority board, is taking ownership of the Housing Action Trust housing and will be responsible for controlling the housing management services in the long term.

Sustaining community-based regeneration

O-Regen and Waltham Forest Housing Action Trust

Waltham Forest Housing Action Trust (WFHAT) was established in 1992, as part of a government initiative to tackle estate regeneration on a comprehensive basis. The Trust is scheduled to wind up in 2002. Covering four high-rise estates in East London, it was home to nearly 6,500 people when work began. WFHAT's primary role has been to undertake a phased redevelopment of the physical fabric, replacing the old housing with predominantly new houses with gardens. But with the community remaining in place throughout the process, a wide range of economic and social programmes have also been established to radically improve residents' quality of life. WFHAT has placed a particular emphasis on community capacity building throughout its programme.

Before its establishment, the local authority provided staff and consultants to work with tenants to develop their expectations and vision of what the Housing Action Trust should do. The involvement of tenants in planning the initiative before it started led directly to a strong sense of ownership of WFHAT by local people, something which has been a lasting and critical factor in the success of the project. WFHAT has just completed a special four-day Citizens' Jury to determine tenants' key priorities to sustain their improved quality of life over the next 10 years.

Tenants have been fully involved throughout WFHAT's life in all major decision making, policy formulation and implementation, right from board level, where they have four places, down to the tenant organisations established on each estate. These bodies are elected annually and have been supported with office facilities, grants and skills training to enable them to fulfil their representative role. They have also been supported by a team of estate-based community development workers.

Also critical to the success of the WFHAT project was having a separate Directorate to 'champion' the cause of community development, but with *all* its departments corporately responsible for tenant involvement and accountability. Housing Action Trusts were set up with a 10-year life linked to substantial budgets. Those involved with them, including tenants, were able to take a long-term view and plan carefully for future sustainability and an appropriate exit strategy.

O-Regen has been set up as a Community Trust and was formerly the Community and Economic Development Department of WFHAT. It is one of two successor bodies which will take over in 2002. O-Regen will take over the ownership of the community buildings and the continued implementation of the community and economic regeneration strategy. The other successor body is the Community Based Housing Association, run by a tenant-majority board, which is currently taking ownership of new WFHAT housing and will be responsible for continued housing management services into the future.

O-Regen has an annual turnover of approximately £2 million. Around £600,000 is spent annually on capacity building programmes, including running the European-funded 'Pathways' programme, a WFHAT contract and community centres.

The financial standing of O-Regen is clearly critical to its future success, and it has been deliberately established as a borough-wide strategic partnership aiming to add value to other regeneration programmes. It has received an initial cash endowment of £2 million from WFHAT, which will continue to underpin the revenue costs of O-Regen until 2001. Long-term sustainability is dependent on drawing in income from endowments, business development, general fundraising, grants and from expanding contract work.

The Waltham Forest initiative is a good example of what can be done given a comprehensive approach to community development and a substantial budget. Unfortunately, Housing Action Trusts are probably too expensive to be replicated elsewhere, but there are many lessons for area regeneration to be learned.

Working at the community's pace

Such approaches clearly take time, resources and commitment, both on the part of the community and the professional agencies providing support. As we have said earlier, not all communities will want to go this far or be able to sustain this level of involvement. They will need support to find their own level and this may well change over time. But, where communities want to take the lead throughout and beyond the regeneration process, they undoubtedly hold the key to the sustainability of their neighbourhoods. They may also be helping to avoid another round of misdirected or wasted resources.

Finally, we consider the issue of representation and coordination. Developing a community-based approach to regeneration has to be addressed at national, regional and local levels. Nationally, it can be tackled through the work of government departments and voluntary sector umbrella bodies; locally through the work of intermediaries, voluntary sector organisations and communities themselves. It is at the regional level where there has, until recently, been an obvious gap.

Resourcing the regions

Community and voluntary sector representation at regional levels is in its infancy. However, a number of Regional Voluntary Sector Networks are now up and running, many supported by funding from the DETR, the Home Office, the National Lottery Charities Board and thematic SRB programmes. They are beginning to make an input into the development of regional strategies for social and economic development, but most are not yet involved in the prioritising of neighbourhoods for area regeneration funding or the wider policy and structural issues concerning neighbourhood regeneration which feed into national debate and policy making. In particular, black communities are often excluded from regeneration because there is no coherent regional organisational structure through which they can present a focused message and negotiate from a position of strength.

There is, perhaps, a role in some regions for new bodies – in the form of regional community agencies. These could be independent, representing a consortium of voluntary sector and community organisations, or attached to a regional body such as the Government Office or RDA. Within different regions there may well be other ways in which representation can be achieved, perhaps through some of the existing voluntary sector networks. However it is done, regional agencies will need help from central government if social and community regeneration issues are not to be overwhelmed by the focus on economic issues in many regions.

Further thought needs to be given to the most appropriate structure for such bodies, along with their role, remit and linkage at local and national levels. Consideration also needs to be given to the representation of black and ethnic minority communities as there is a severe lack of black agencies operating at regional levels and white-led agencies are not effective substitutes.

Resourcing resident-controlled neighbourhood regeneration

Royds Community Association, Bradford

Royds Community Association set out eight years ago to regenerate three local authority housing estates in south west Bradford. Its overall aim was to build self-sustaining communities, with residents centrally involved in identifying their future needs and actively involved in meeting them. A small, but determined group including a private sector individual, a local authority housing officer, and several local residents, spent three years preparing detailed plans and proposals before a major SRB bid was submitted.

£30 million of SRB resources are now being invested in social, economic and physical development across three estates, but Royds is no ordinary estate regeneration initiative. On the contrary, it is now nationally recognised as one of the country's most successful resident-led estate regeneration intiatives.

The Royds Board has 22 directors, including 12 who are elected locally. Most of its committees and groups are chaired by local people. Significantly, Royds Community Association is the accountable body for SRB purposes, something which was successfully negotiated with the City Council at the start of the programme. Local people therefore have control of the regeneration programme, working in close partnership with other agencies.

An extensive programme of support and training is provided for local residents, enabling the local communities to be centrally involved at all levels of the organisation. Around £400,000 is spent annually on community capacity building, in addition to the capital investment in two new community centres which are already self-sufficent financially. A Social Action programme, launched in 1998, aims to have more than 100 residents involved in voluntary work on the estates by 2002.

The impact of this high level of investment can be seen in many areas of estate life. Police records for the area show that juvenile crime was reduced to almost zero during the period of summer programmes provided by Royds in 1998.

However, it is the strong emphasis on resident-controlled asset creation which is particularly notable. The Community Association currently owns land transferred to them by the local authority as well as a number of community facilities. It plans to invest capital receipts from land sales in order to generate income and make it completely financially independent of local authority support by the end of the SRB programme.

5

An overview of current practice

The resourcing role

There are many organisations, operating at national, regional and local level, which have a direct role in resourcing community capacity building. The plethora of agencies and funding programmes and the complicated nature of their funding conditions has contributed to a patchwork of support which is, as yet, not comprehensive or well coordinated. Accessing resources for community capacity building is, as a result, not always as straightforward as it should be. Although not an exhaustive list, the main elements of the patchwork are summarised in this chapter.

Central government

Central government has taken a strong lead in ensuring that its own area-based programmes give community capacity building a high priority. It provides direct funding, particularly through the SRB and New Deal for Communities programmes. While the latter is focused initially on 17 Pathfinder neighbourhoods, with a three-year budget of £800 million, the former is now being targeted on larger areas, with a three-year budget of £1.3 billion. A total of 20% of the SRB5 budget is reserved for regeneration projects which fall outside those areas prioritised by the Local Index of Deprivation (DETR, 1998a).

Central government departments, primarily the DETR and the Home Office, also fund intermediaries involved in promoting community-based regeneration through advice on best practice, funding local projects through loans and grants and meeting the training needs of voluntary workers. New programmes

designed primarily to tackle social exclusion in deprived neighbourhoods have resources for capacity building built into them, including Health, Education and Employment Action Zones and Sure Start.

Within the regions, Government Offices retain responsibility for monitoring public expenditure and a number of government programmes, including New Deal for Communities.

Government sponsored agencies

Regional Development Agencies

The new RDAs have a strong focus on economic investment. It is uncertain how many of them, if any, will develop a strategic approach to social and community regeneration, so funding support for community capacity building, other than through SRB programmes, is likely to be limited, at least in the short term. The Community Investment Fund, a useful source of capital finance for a range of community projects and previously operated by English Partnerships, has now been transferred to the RDAs and is no longer a ring-fenced budget.

The Housing Corporation

The Housing Corporation is responsible for the funding and regulation of housing associations in England, many of whom have a substantial stake in deprived urban neighbourhoods through their ownership and management of social housing. A total of 60% of the Corporation's capital funding programme was spent on area regeneration projects in 1998/99. Although some associations have been very proactive in supporting community-based initiatives, most notably those involved in People for Action 2001, many mainstream associations have been wary of moving beyond their traditional role as housing providers. This now looks set to change.

The recent Housing Corporation decision to extend the 'permissible purposes' of housing associations has enabled some of them to begin operating as broadly-based neighbourhood regeneration agencies. They will shortly be backed by Corporation grants specifically for community capacity building and sustainability work. The growing role for housing associations in community investment is the subject of a recent JRF publication (Dwelly, 1999).

Community Development Foundation

The Community Development Foundation, which is a charity sponsored by the Home Office, provides support for a wide range of community initiatives and specialises in advice on community development. Among its many activities, the Foundation runs capacity building grants programmes, mainly aimed at helping community groups to learn from each other.

Training and Enterprise Councils

Training and Enterprise Councils (TECs) are locally-based companies with employer-led boards. Their remit has been to coordinate the delivery of training and business support within their areas, but they are shortly to be replaced by the new Skills Councils. Some TECs have been placing an emphasis on capacity building programmes for community businesses, primarily as partners in SRB initiatives, but this has always been a very small part of their business.

Health authorities

Regional health authorities have a similarly small, but growing role in community capacity building. Health Action Zones have resources for capacity building and community development work, as do the new Primary Care Groups.

Regional Arts Boards

Regional Arts Boards also have a small role in capacity building, through their support for a range of community arts programmes.

Local authorities

Local authorities have traditionally had a key role in resourcing community capacity building, primarily through the provision of grants to community organisations, the running of community centres and the employment of community development workers. While non-financial forms of support are still much in evidence, and local authorities are playing a leading role in most SRB and New Deal for Communities Programmes, funding restrictions have substantially reduced their ability to sustain grant programmes and this has had a significant impact on community involvement. Strategic partnerships with other funders have helped to plug some of the more obvious gaps.

Local authorities do now have access to £12 million of DETR funding, spread over two years, for Tenant Participation Compacts. This initiative is specifically designed to capacity build tenants' organisations and enable them to play a key role in Best Value, particularly in those areas where participation has been slow to get off the ground. If used to supplement voluntary efforts by tenants to involve themselves in training and networking, this fund could play an important role in capacity building many communities unable to benefit from area regeneration funding.

European Funding Programmes

The European Union provides important funding for local projects involved in community-based regeneration.

European Regional Development Fund

The current round of the European Regional Development Fund came to an end in 1999 and has been used to support a wide range of projects in priority areas, some involving the development of local community partnerships, community training and a range of self-help projects. Community involvement will, however, be a more explicit theme of the 2000-06 Structural Fund programme.

URBAN

The URBAN Initiative, funded through the European Regional Development Fund, is specifically targeted on community capacity building in inner-city communities and also concluded in 1999. Key themes included improving information and communication within local communities and supporting the development and capacity of community organisations.

European Social Fund

The European Social Fund's (ESF) Objective 3, Priority 4 Programme is currently being used to build the capacity of small, locally-based organisations involved in community training and job creation initiatives. This is a relatively new aspect of ESF programmes, which have, in the past, mainly concerned themselves with mainstream training for unemployed individuals. A total of 4% of the UK ESF budget was set aside for capacity building local community organisations within this programme.

All European funding programmes carry with them problems of long lead-in times and particular difficulties with matching funding, which continue to pose serious problems for local communities trying to access them. But some solutions to these problems are now being tested.

National Lottery programmes

National Lottery Charities Board

The National Lottery Charities Board is the largest grant-making body in Britain. The main themes of its annual £350 million programme, administered on a regional basis, are community involvement, and poverty and disadvantage. In consequence, many of its grants support a broad range of community capacity building initiatives in deprived urban neighbourhoods. It also operates a small grants programme – Awards for All – which provides amounts of between £500 and £5,000 for smaller-scale capacity building activities, with no deadlines or priority themes.

The Board embarked on a regional capacity building programme for the voluntary and community sectors in late 1999.

New Opportunities Fund

One of the four key objectives of the New Opportunities Fund is to encourage community participation and ownership. It expects to work in close collaboration with other funders, particularly the Charities Board and does not expect to be a main source of funding for capacity building. Nevertheless, the Healthy Living Centre initiative (£300 million) might, as part of the overall project costs, provide some funding for community capacity building, although other partners will normally be expected to fund this at the project development stage. Similarly, the Fund's £400 million Out of School Hours Education and Childcare Initiative may fund an element of capacity building, again as part of project costs.

Arts Council of England

The Arts Council runs its own lottery programme as well as providing grant-in-aid to arts-based organisations. Since late 1998, the focus of its lottery capital programme has shifted to projects in deprived areas and this is likely to be a stronger feature of its future programme. Half the awards within the Arts for Everyone small grants programme now go to locally-based voluntary or community groups.

Community and voluntary sector intermediary agencies

Intermediary organisations

Intermediary organisations provide a range of facilities and resources specifically targeted at increasing the capacity of community groups. They can offer advice, support and expertise. They can provide resources, such as office equipment, management support, advice on organisational structures and financial systems, training and information courses, and access to information on funding, legal and technical issues. They offer opportunities for community groups to network, thus sharing skills, information and enabling joint working. They can provide a developmental role, assisting with the establishment of new groups, giving ongoing support to others and supporting voluntary activity in communities. They can raise issues of race and gender and help ensure that groups operate on the basis of equality. Some offer technical services, such as community planning and architecture.

Intermediaries involved in neighbourhood regeneration include technical aid organisations, settlements, social action centres, housing associations, development trusts and private sector consultancies. Some are subsidiaries of larger organisations. There are also individuals and consultancy organisations specialising in the field which can offer a range of services.

A broad range of community and voluntary sector agencies are involved in resourcing community capacity building, either directly or through a network of intermediaries. Those most directly involved in capacity building in urban neighbourhoods include the following.

Development Trusts Association

The Development Trusts Association (DTA) has 264 member organisations in England and is organised on a regional basis. It manages two small funds with a capacity building focus: an Asset Base Development Fund, financed through DETR's Special Grants programme, which requires a 50% contribution from applicants; and a Knowledge and Skills Exchange, funded by the Baring Foundation. Both are aimed at equipping communities with the understanding they need to take forward proposals for establishing Development Trusts. DTA is also a partner in an innovative European project in South Yorkshire – the South Yorkshire Key Fund – which has managed to avoid the problems of matched funding so often experienced by community organisations and regeneration initiatives.

Community Matters

Community Matters – the nationwide federation of community organisations, with nearly 1,000 members – runs a community consultancy service using experienced practitioners within its network to work with community groups to help build their capacity. It is also currently promoting the piloting of Community Technical Assistance Vouchers.

Councils for Voluntary Service

The 250 local Councils for Voluntary Service provide an important resource for local communities and often play an important role in capacity building, primarily through the provision of information, advice and training.

They are supported by the National Association of Councils for Voluntary Service, funded mainly by the Home Office and DETR.

British Association of Settlements and Social Action Centres

The British Association of Settlements and Social Action Centres is a national organisation with a network of 78 members, focusing on locally-based multi-purpose centres involved in helping deprived communities bring about social change.

Black Training and Enterprise Group

The Black Training and Enterprise Group (BTEG) is a national black organisation established in 1991 by representatives from the black voluntary sector. It contributes to the economic regeneration of black communities in the UK and represents over 200 organisations. BTEG focuses on training, employment, enterprise and regeneration.

Urban Forum

Urban Forum is the only national voluntary organisation specialising in urban regeneration. Since 1994, it has been representing the sector nationally on area regeneration issues and has played a key role in securing resources for community capacity building through both the SRB and New Deal for Communities programmes.

A number of other national organisations provide information and advice to enable local urban communities to access resources. They include the Church Urban Fund, the Standing Conference on Community Development and the National Association of Volunteer Bureaux. The newly established Regional Voluntary Sector Networks are also expected to play an important role in capacity building work.

Private trusts and foundations

There are many trusts and foundations which support community-based initiatives, ranging from well-known national bodies, such as the Baring, Calouste Gulbenkian and Joseph Rowntree Foundations, to small local charities with limited grant-giving roles. Few of them have a particular focus on regeneration and most wish to see tangible outputs for their investment – something to which community capacity building work is not well suited. Consequently, not enough money is getting down to where it really counts. Nevertheless, considerable investment is going into helping intermediaries build their capacity, both internally and through developing networks.

The Association of Community Trusts and Foundations represents private trusts and foundations. It supports a growing network of 24 community foundations which between them now make local grants of around £13 million per annum and hold endowment funds of more than £65 million, raised primarily from individuals, private and charitable donations.

Area regeneration programmes

The most significant resources for community capacity building in deprived urban neighbourhoods come through two government flagship programmes – the Single Regeneration Budget and New Deal for Communities. Virtually all SRB initiatives are now expected to include provision for community capacity building, with up to 10% of project resources devoted to this activity over their lifetime. The Round 5 programme introduced, for the first time, the possibility of funding specifically to enable communities to be centrally involved in bid preparation. DETR advice in this area was very clear.

> Deprived areas do not always have well-established and effective partnerships or well-mobilised communities. This can stand in the way of their securing much-needed funding.... In areas where there are no significant regeneration programmes which could accommodate local capacity building activity, the Government is prepared to consider free-standing bids devoted to capacity building. Such bids must include proposals [a forward strategy] for the development and delivery of sustainable projects which would flow from the capacity building phase. (DETR, 1998b, Section 3.8)

DETR advice given to New Deal for Communities Pathfinders on the preparation of their delivery plans also placed great emphasis on the need to capacity build communities at all levels and at all stages of the process.

> Partnerships should ensure that projects to promote and develop the community's capacity to contribute to the regeneration and development of their neighbourhood are reflected in the Delivery Plans, and remain a priority throughout the lifetime of regeneration schemes. A particular problem may be that community representatives lack the experience or support other members of the partnership take for granted. Resources made available through the second phase of NDC will help to build the capacity of the community. This may involve training community representatives, providing support workers to help the community develop skills, or providing access to administrative or office resources. (DETR, 1999, Chapter 4)

Capacity building – an encouraging start

Work to build the capacity of communities living in priority deprived urban neighbourhoods appears to be increasing dramatically. Local authorities and other stakeholders are clearly responding positively to the government's lead.

An initial appraisal of DETR's Successful Bids Document for Round 5 of the SRB programme, announced in July 1999, illustrates the point. Of the 163 approved projects, just over half (86) have community capacity building among their key outputs. Nearly two thirds of these are area- or neighbourhood-based programmes. They propose to deliver no less than 3,277 capacity building initiatives during their lifetime – an average of 61 separate initiatives per project (see Table 1).

With lifetime SRB funding of over £500 million for these projects, it is reasonable to assume that at least £50 million is being invested in neighbourhood- or area-based community capacity building through this round of the SRB programme. With most area-based programmes running for between five and seven years, this amounts to an annual spend of around £8 million a year.

Table 1: Community capacity building within the SRB5 programme, by region

	East	East Midlands	London	North East	North West	South East	South West	West Midlands	Yorkshire/ Humberside	Total
Total SRB5 initiatives	11	11	38	16	23	24	8	18	14	163
SRB lifetime spend (£m)	20,556	64,030	319,759	119,631	217,809	70,358	30,917	87,242	108,763	1,039,065
Area-based iniatives with CCBPs*	6	1	13	4	17	5	4	1†	4	61
Lifetime SRB spend on these initiatives (£m)	8,298	13,000	153,003	34,229	195,158	8,662	17,019	4,460	67,109	500,937
Number of CCBPs	231	47	787	84	1,323	129	53	31‡	592‡	3,277
Average CCBPs per initiative	38	47	60	21	78	26	13	31	53§	61

Notes: CCBPs (community capacity building projects);
* taken from bid 'key outputs';
† likely to be under-represented, but regional emphasis appears to be on personal and social development;
‡ includes one major programme in Leeds with 432 CCBPs;
§ excludes Leeds capacity building initiative.

Source: DETR SRB5 Successful Bids, July 1999

Regional variations

There are, however, some interesting regional variations. Two thirds of the community capacity building initiatives are in London and the North West. While the latter has secured 21% of the SRB5 resources, it has no less than 40% of the community capacity building initiatives talking place across the country. The North East, on the other hand, having secured 11.5% of the programme, can only muster 2.5% of the capacity building initiatives.

However, it may be sensible to exercise some caution with these figures. Research on previous rounds of the SRB programme has suggested that the number of capacity building projects included in bids can be a poor guide to both the quantity and quality of projects actually delivered in local communities.

The take-up of SRB resources for community capacity building prior to a full bid has not, so far, been substantial. Of the 163 approved Round 5 bids, only six fall into this category. All these projects are in southern England and the East Midlands, with a combined budget of just under £2.5 million.

There is clearly a much greater emphasis on community capacity building in some parts of the country than there is in others. It is hard to escape the conclusion that most of the SRB5 resources for community capacity building are going to regions which already have a reasonably strong track record of involving communities in area-based regeneration. Regions with a more limited track record in this field appear to be lagging behind, perhaps reflecting a more traditional or paternalistic approach among many of their key players.

In the South East, London and the East Midlands, three SRB5 projects are attempting to build the capacity of communities and voluntary sector intermediaries through establishing and supporting new regional networks. One of them is specifically focused on equipping local communities with the skills they need to mount their own bids for regeneration funding.

There are, as yet, very few examples of local communities actually taking the lead in regeneration partnerships; it will take time for the new emphasis on capacity building to work its way through to a point where this becomes the rule rather than the exception. Capacity building a regional network of intermediaries, particularly in those parts of the country with a relatively low level of community involvement in regeneration, could make an important contribution here.

Questionnaire survey of area regeneration initiatives

Part of the research for this study included a small questionnaire survey of area regeneration initiatives, some of them long-established and funded from a variety of sources. We deliberately targeted those projects which had a capacity building focus, taking advice from regional Government Offices on those we selected. We wanted to find out what resources they had invested in community capacity building, what specific activities they had supported and what practical difficulties they had experienced. We found a generally positive picture. (The Appendix lists those organisations which participated in the questionnaire survey.)

Getting the community involved early

It is now widely accepted that getting the local community involved early can have a significant impact on the long-term sustainability of any area regeneration initiative. However, less than a third of the initiatives we surveyed had attempted to involve local communities in drawing up their initial delivery plans. Those that had done so were mainly supported by community development workers, backed up by limited funding for community consultation on the bid, both provided by local authorities. In just one case had an SRB bid been preceded by the production of a community strategy or plan.

Pressures of funding timetables and the lack of resources for pre-bid consultation obviously played a part, but there remains a culture – particularly in many local authorities – that professionals prepare bids and then involve communities in implementation. Capacity building communities to prepare their own bids, as leaders or key partners, is breaking new ground even with those regeneration agencies with a strong track record in community-based regeneration.

Investment in community capacity building

These initiatives spent, on average, £200,000 a year on community capacity building, or around 15% of their total expenditure. Interestingly, this is higher than the government's current 10% limit for community capacity building within SRB programmes, but this can be explained partly by the inclusion in the survey of non-SRB projects, such as the European Commission's URBAN Initiative and Housing Action Trusts, both of which have substantial budgets for this type of work. We did, however, find a very broad range. Some initiatives were investing between 20% and 45% of their budgets on capacity building work, while others were limiting themselves to between 1.5% and 5%. Figure 1 shows the range.

Figure 1: Annual expenditure by area regeneration iniatives on capacity building (%)

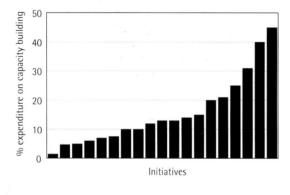

Type of capacity building projects supported

The range of community capacity building projects undertaken within these area regeneration initiatives was considerable. Figure 2 illustrates this range and the most popular approaches. Developing the effectiveness of local intermediaries, community development work with existing community groups and ensuring that communities played an active role in regeneration partnerships were the activities prioritised by most initiatives. Work in these fields no doubt led on to support for some of the more specific projects.

Funding sources

There is a heavy reliance on mainstream regeneration funding for capacity building work, which is perhaps inevitable. The SRB, the European programmes and local authorities were the main sources of support. Nevertheless, the initiatives have, between them, managed to attract funding from 19 different sources – no mean achievement for activities where quantifiable outputs are notoriously difficult to pin down. Only a handful of community capacity building projects had failed to take off or been aborted due to lack of funding, mainly the result of failed European bids or changed priorities within the partnerships themselves.

Figure 2: Range of community capacity building projects supported by area regeneration iniatives

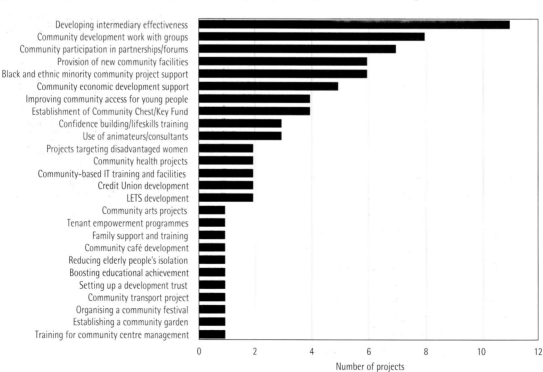

Figure 3 illustrates the range and popularity of funding sources.

Non-financial support

Successful community capacity building requires much more than an injection of finance. Indeed, what local communities often need most in their early stages is support, training, basic equipment and space in which to carry out their activities. The commitment of time from professionals, acting as enablers, is particularly important – something which most of the initiatives we surveyed recognised early on. Figure 4 sets out the range and popularity of the non-financial support offered to communities.

To be fully sustainable in the long term, there needs to be a shift from enabling to empowering; from professional support to staff secondments and funding for direct employment by communities of their own staff. Only a handful of the initiatives we surveyed had reached this stage and it was not clear whether this was a future priority for all of the others.

Boosting community skills

No amount of finance, equipment and support can hope to strengthen the capacity of communities unless local people gain new skills, experience and the confidence to manage their own affairs. Regeneration partnerships have rightly prioritised this type of work. Figure 5 illustrates the main areas of community skilling work which have been undertaken. Other types of training support have included organisational development, project management, strategic planning, networking and understanding jargon and systems.

Community-based succession strategies

The real test of successful capacity building within area regeneration initiatives lies in how much community involvement there is in the succession strategy. Some of the initiatives we looked at had put considerable resources into ensuring that communities had a real stake – and sometimes a controlling stake – in these vehicles. They had helped to create new community-led organisations, to take the initiative forward once mainstream funding had run out, with endowments of land, buildings and

Figure 3: Source of funding for capacity building projects undertaken by area regeneration initiatives

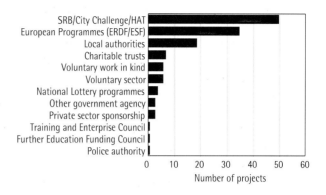

Figure 4: Non-financial forms of capacity building support

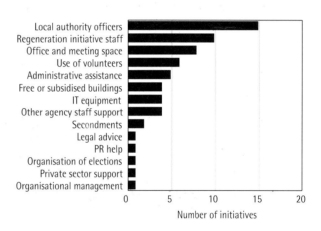

Figure 5: Targeting community skills

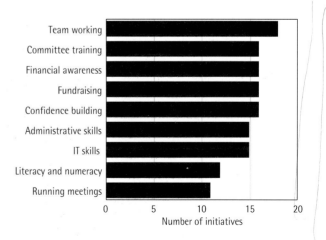

capital to sustain the initiative well beyond the life of the regeneration programme. Development trusts were generally the most popular model.

However, establishing new vehicles was not widely adopted. More than half of the other initiatives had decided to pass continuing work over to an existing community-based agency or local intermediary.

Summarising the lessons

The main lessons for resourcing which can be drawn from these area regeneration initiatives are as follows.

- No significant resources are yet being deployed for community involvement in bid preparation, either through the production of community plans or other mechanisms.
- More time is needed at the front end of neighbourhood regeneration programmes to capacity build communities effectively.
- There is no real shortage of financial resources for community capacity building within current area regeneration programmes.
- Community development work is not currently being prioritised as a specific activity in many programmes.
- There is only limited evidence that regeneration programmes have successfully moved from enabling to empowering communities during their lifetime.
- Most agencies place more emphasis on resourcing community involvement in the process of regeneration than they do in the programmes and the products.

Despite these important lessons, those communities which have successfully attracted regeneration funding and the associated non-financial resources have, in the main, at least had their problems ameliorated, if not fully resolved. Nevertheless, there remain significant gaps to be filled. There are many other deprived neighbourhoods which have not yet been able to attract regeneration funding, either because they fall outside statistical indictors of need, or have communities with no experience of lobbying for resources. While there are certainly significant gaps in the way we resource community involvement in area regeneration programmes,

these are compounded in those communities which have difficulty in accessing any resources at all.

At a strategic level, we must ensure that:

- the resources available for neighbourhood regeneration are used more effectively;
- new ways are found to bend mainstream programmes and services and focus attention on deprived communities;
- pressure is applied on those agencies responsible for regeneration to ensure they deliver a more community-centred agenda.

In short, we must not only fill the gaps, we must also re-focus the programmes and those responsible for delivering them.

These are significant challenges and they need to be set within the emerging national strategy for neighbourhood renewal (SEU, 1998). How we resource communities must be a central element in this strategy. Chapters 6 and 7 examine how this might be achieved.

6

A strategic approach to filling the gaps

A strategic approach to resourcing community involvement must be delivered at a number of different levels – regional, city-wide and within neighbourhoods themselves. The national strategy for neighbourhood renewal (SEU, 1998) will provide both the framework and the starting point. To be effective, it will need to:

- highlight the importance of neighbourhood management as the key means of achieving neighbourhood renewal at local level;
- place community involvement and capacity building at the centre of the neighbourhood management approach;
- successfully join-up neighbourhood management with city-wide, sub-regional and regional strategies.

As Marilyn Taylor correctly asserts in her forthcoming report on neighbourhood management:

> If neighbourhood management is to make a difference where other initiatives have failed, everyone – from communities to local authorities – needs to be convinced, firstly, that it is different from what has gone before and, secondly, that it is worth the considerable energies and costs that will be involved. Bringing excluded areas in from the cold will mean getting rid of old ways of doing things and taking risks. It is unlikely to be a comfortable ride. (Taylor, 2000)

The focus on neighbourhoods and a new central role for communities has many implications for those involved and for the way in which future resources are deployed.

- The culture within many of the institutions and agencies responsible for neighbourhood regeneration will need to change.
- New and more appropriate structures for local management will need to emerge.
- Training, for both communities and professionals, will need to be prioritised.
- New evaluation methods will be needed.
- A strategic approach to intermediary agencies will be required.

Changing institutional cultures and capacity

Many of those consulted for this report talked about the need for cultural change within professional organisations, and particularly local authorities, health authorities and housing associations. There was a strong view that while community involvement now appears as a priority in the strategies, programmes and services of many agencies, this rarely reflects the integration of a community-based approach into the ethos of the organisation. Instead, the impressive commitments made in publicity and information are all too often window-dressing and have not been backed up by thorough-going institutional reform. Communities are expected to work hard and to commit voluntary time and effort in order to become able to engage with professional organisations. The expectation that the same is required of the professional organisations is both recent and undeveloped – capacity building both will take time.

Most agencies involved in regeneration, and local government in particular, are dominated by professional groupings such as architects, planners, social workers, housing managers and accountants. These professionals have significant operational power and control of resources. For communities in deprived areas, who most depend upon these services, this power can be experienced as control exercised by others over their lives. They are usually perceived as 'gate-keepers' of resources. It is hardly surprising, therefore, that there is almost always a division between the residents of deprived areas dependent on agencies for services and the officers who run these services. This is clearly not conducive to involving communities in the regeneration of their neighbourhoods.

Prioritising community involvement

Reform is essential if there is to be effective and ongoing community involvement in and influencing of organisations, agencies and local authorities involved in regeneration. Community involvement has to be supported at the highest levels in organisations, including boards, committees and senior management. The front-line staff delivering the organisation's strategies and services need to be, and/or have access to, key decision makers at strategic and operational levels in the organisation. All aspects of community involvement should be prioritised for board/committee consideration. The implications of a community-based approach needs thinking through for the organisation's structure and ways of working. Organisations should involve partner agencies in looking at the implications of a community-based approach for the partnerships and their own organisations.

Essentially, this is about building institutional capacity to plan and deliver a community-based approach to neighbourhood regeneration. It is as vital a component to achieving sustainable regeneration of the poorest neighbourhoods as is building the capacity of the communities themselves. Communities need, at the very least, to be met half way. All the capacity building in the world will count for very little if doors are not open and those who have access to the money and power are not listening.

Modernising local government

Clearly, the requirement that agencies and local authorities address cultural and organisational change within neighbourhood regeneration is closely related to the government's proposals for modernising local government. The need for democratic renewal and greater public involvement are key elements of the changes proposed by the government in its White Paper, *Modernising local government* (DETR, 1998c). The perception that a hearts and minds commitment to community involvement has not been integrated into the ethos of most local authorities is directly related to the low regard in which local people seem to hold their councils.

This is illustrated all too clearly in low levels of engagement and, in particular, poor turnout at local elections. Too many people do not see local government as relevant to their lives. Instead they see an overly-bureaucratic structure peopled by inaccessible officers, the aim of which too often appears to be to keep them (the public) at bay. They see "councillors whose age and gender do not match those of their public and who do not have a high profile or regard in the community" (Filkin et al, 1999).

The Best Value agenda

The government's Best Value agenda seeks to change this. Developing a stronger relationship with its public is central to local government's future and cultures and structures will have to change if this agenda is to be met. There will be a need for

> ... local authorities to set up a systematic approach to develop participation in the council and to embed it throughout the organisation ... [it will require] leadership, professionalism and resources and an infrastructure that leads to real community influence on decision making. (Filkin et al, 1999)

There is a requirement for community plans which will set out a framework for the provision of local services by councils and provide the context for bids to central government. This offers the opportunity to measure the extent to which local authorities have involved their communities in the process and established a systematic approach to further develop participation in the council and to embed it throughout the organisation. Community plans clearly need to be linked to community involvement in neighbourhood regeneration. Community development staff are an obvious

Community planning of neighbourhood-based services

Walsall's Empowering Local Communities Programme

In April 1996 SRB2 funding was awarded to Walsall to fund it's 'Empowering Local Communities' programme. This brought £14.6 million to seven areas of the Borough where capacity building has enabled locally-elected committees to be developed, actively engaging local residents in the prioritisation and planning of statutory agency service provision.

Following consultation, each area was divided into 'patches' of approximately 100 households based on 'natural' community boundaries. In November 1997 democratic elections were held for each 'patch'. All residents aged 16 and over were eligible to vote. In one of the areas, telephone voting was piloted in partnership with British Telecom. Young people had a right to elect two youth representatives to each committee. Walsall Council identified lead officers to work with each committee, acting as an interface between the committee and the Council.

In December 1997 local committees held their first meetings. Officers were elected and constitutions developed. Committees vary in size from 15 to 30 resident representatives, and make decisions on SRB projects, influence Council mainstream funding and have a key role in Best Value. Some capacity building funding is directly controlled by local committees, for example, Community Chest funds, but the emphasis here is on policy, planning and influence of mainstream Council budgets rather than direct control of resources.

The local authority currently manages the election process to local committees, and finances those outside the SRB2 area. Local committees have now developed a momentum which will continue to receive support from major agencies following completion of the SRB2 programme.

Approximately 13% of the annual budget (£330,000) is spent on capacity building activity, with SRB funding supplemented by European Regional Development Funding. Outcomes achieved include the establishment of seven locally-elected committees with greater involvement of residents in project management and implementation. Additional local committees are now being established using SRB4 funding.

A number of factors seem to have been critical to the success of the work in Walsall, including the support and goodwill of politicians, plus drive and commitment from senior officers. Together these factors generated a corporate culture supportive of local accountability. Other factors included top-level support for local authority officers working at the interface between local committees and the authority, and the willingness to integrate community planning into corporate priorities.

Just as significantly, the Empowering Local Communities Programme has laid a strong foundation for future community-led area regeneration in Walsall.

access point for the new relationship between communities and modern, open government.

Finally, the New Commitment to Regeneration, launched by the Local Government Association, will attempt to integrate area regeneration programmes with mainstream services and programmes, thus moving away from a competitive process. The lessons learned from the 22 Pathfinder areas developing the approach will be fed into the neighbourhood regeneration agenda. With the emphasis on local

determination and local delivery there could be policy and practice lessons relevant to community involvement in neighbourhood regeneration.

While local authorities are at the front-line of this, other agencies cannot afford to be complacent. We found clear evidence that housing associations, TECs, health authorities and other statutory organisations are equally in need of such reform. Professional capacity building is as important in these organisations as it is in local authorities. The assumptions, analyses and requirements of the Best Value agenda in the White Paper should be applied by these organisations to their own cultures, structures and services. In addition, internal training and developmental work specifically focused on extending community involvement in area regeneration in order to build capacity should be addressed as part of this wider agenda.

Building voluntary sector capacity

Building the capacity of the voluntary sector is the next part of the equation. Many of the organisations contributing to this report identified the tensions often evident between the voluntary sector and community groups. While all acknowledged that there are clear differences between the two it was felt that these differences too often become a cause for conflict rather than the foundation of a creative partnership. Differences of control, funding, function, resources and organisation can lead to difficulties and sometimes resentment. Such differences are exacerbated by external pressures. The recent proliferation of new initiatives, programmes, funding regimes and policies highlight these problems.

The voluntary sector needs to build its capacity in order to enable greater community participation, deliver services and support that are appropriate to the changing needs of communities and generally move towards a greater level of accountability. They need to be better able to meet new challenges and demands for new services. In addition, many voluntary organisations need strengthening generally, through improvements in administration, marketing, financial systems and fundraising.

Applying sanctions

Finally, careful consideration needs to be given to the application of sanctions. If we accept that effective and long-lasting regeneration of some of our poorest neighbourhoods cannot be achieved without significant changes taking place within the institutions and agencies involved, sanctions will be necessary if this change does not take place. At national and regional levels of government there is currently a marked reluctance to apply effective measures. Too often agencies are given more time to get

things right, or worse, given more money. The majority of institutions change as a result of pressure from the top-down or the bottom-up; only those that are particularly creative and dynamic can self-generate and manage reform. Communities, particularly as a result of capacity building, can exert pressure, but they need help from government to achieve the required effect. They also need to be protected from the implications of any financial sanctions imposed on agencies for under-performance.

New structures for local management

The new emphasis on neighbourhood management will mean that, in many cases, the wider area partnership boards of City Challenge and SRB programmes will be replaced by more localised neighbourhood boards. These will involve residents, public and private sector agencies and other interested parties in much the same way as partnership boards do currently. The new boards will employ staff who will form a multi-disciplinary project team appropriate to the particular needs of the neighbourhood. This is in direct contrast to the programme-based teams which characterise current area regeneration, such as Sure Start, Education Action Zones, and Health Action Zones.

Neighbourhood teams

The neighbourhood teams will need a clear link into wider-area and city regeneration programmes and mainstream services. A workable, effective and transparent structure will be essential in order to maximise the impact of neighbourhood regeneration programmes and their contribution to city-wide regeneration strategies.

On the ground, staffing structures within neighbourhood teams must give priority to community development posts. Community development workers are the most prevalent and important form of support that communities can access. Their role is explicitly geared towards supporting, advising and developing community groups. They have the capacity and skills to develop in-depth knowledge about localities and the needs of residents. Such local familiarity and presence can lead to close and productive relationships with communities, based on trust and mutual respect.

Community development workers

Community development workers should therefore be seen as the main resource for supporting existing and developing new community groups, developing and supporting voluntary activity, offering specialist skills in capacity building and encouraging resident involvement in participative structures. All these activities are essential features in establishing community involvement in neighbourhood regeneration programmes. Put simply, community development is the most effective resource for encouraging comprehensive planning and joint working between agencies which is led from the bottom-up.

However, some changes are essential. Many of the traditional skills, attributes and approaches are still valid, but new ones are needed. We need to define the new skills and areas of expertise required of community development workers in neighbourhood management – a rare combination of skills is required. They include:

- community development approaches and methods, focused on enabling people to achieve things themselves and strengthen their abilities;
- entrepreneurialism;
- the ability to engage at different levels of government;
- an understanding of the work of different sectors and an ability to work across them;
- knowledge of a wide variety of funding sources and the ability to access them;
- the ability to mobilise a range of agencies and resources to target appropriate action where it is most needed;
- a strong commitment to the neighbourhood and its residents.

The primary tasks for community development staff within neighbourhood regeneration teams will therefore be to work with the community to identify priorities, develop a community vision or plan, establish consultative and participatory structures and implement a comprehensive programme of support and resources for community-based activity and projects through a capacity building plan.

Prioritising training

While effective capacity building necessitates a wide range of approaches and methods, training is clearly one of the most important. Our research showed that further work needs to be done on forms of appropriate and accessible training for communities. As in other areas of capacity building, a more rigorous approach to delivery is required. Programmes should be based on training needs assessments which identify gaps. Such assessments should be carried out by the community, with the necessary support, and take account of gender and race differences. Training should be related not only to the particular demands of the neighbourhood regeneration programme, but also to the pre-existing needs of individuals and groups.

A wide variety of forms of training are necessary in capacity building. Residents start at different levels, they learn in different ways and they want to gain knowledge and skills in different areas. Traditional course-based training is but one form among a wide range of others which include mentoring, action-based learning, placements and group-based training.

In terms of specific areas for training, three in particular emerged from the research for this study. The first is training in accessing funding. Recent research by The Arts Council suggests that community groups face difficulties in accessing their lottery funds due to a lack of relevant training. These problems are particularly marked among certain black groups. The Confederation of Indian Organisations supported this view and also emphasised the need for leadership development for black groups.

Second, training needs to be specifically targeted at enabling residents to access paid jobs in regeneration, something which can be an essential component of long-term neighbourhood sustainability.

Third, training is particularly important for residents involved in partnership boards and sub-groups or committees. Several of those interviewed talked not only about the need for initial training, but also for ongoing support throughout the period of board membership.

New evaluation methods

There is wide consensus on the need for evaluation of capacity building projects and community involvement structures in area regeneration programmes – that is, a thorough process of assessing effectiveness against stated objectives. However, current evaluation approaches and processes often lack rigour and are inappropriate. A number of problems have emerged from the research.

Evaluations are often carried out internally by people with a vested interest in the projects and programmes. The measurements used are not always appropriate and/or relevant, and are rarely agreed with the community. They are not always rigorous enough to really establish the financial efficiency and tangible efficacy of capacity building programmes, yet the process and intrusion can seem interminable. They are not used as effectively as they could be to identify and address poor practice.

So, how should evaluation of community capacity building take place? Who should do it and how should it be used in terms of dissemination? Guidance on appropriate measures and indicators and implementing a more rigorous approach can be found in the significant amount of literature now available on evaluating community involvement and capacity building (see, for example, Barr et al, 1996; Chanan et al, 1999; Skinner, 1997). A number of organisations, including JRF, the New Economics Foundation and Urban Forum, are helping to develop new evaluative tools.

However, we would like to highlight one key issue. Evaluative measures applied to black communities usually use the term 'ethnic minorities'. This generalises and thus obscures the impact of regeneration programmes upon particular groups, such as Afro-Caribbean, Pakistani or Bangladeshi communities. It is impossible to ascertain whether resources and benefits are effectively targeting those black communities most in need. It is therefore necessary to monitor by specific racial origin.

Evaluating the impact of community involvement

Evaluation which takes account of community involvement should be carried out at key points in the process of area regeneration. There are various stages at which a greater or lesser level of evaluation could be usefully applied. This could be:

- at the end of the bid process, in order to ascertain the quality and quantity of community involvement in the process;
- at the conclusion of the development of the delivery plan, to assess the proposed programme in terms of its impact on and benefit to the local communities;
- at the point at which the participatory and partnership structures have been set up, in order to establish the consultative and decision-making processes involved and the consequent level of participation by the community;
- at the end of each substantive project, be it a capacity building or a capital project, in order to learn lessons and develop guidance for future projects;
- at the end of each year of the programme, to review progress and develop guidelines for the next period.

Whichever stage is evaluated, a key criteria in the evaluation should be the effect on the local communities.

Currently, the majority of evaluation is undertaken by professional staff involved in the programme. We would argue for a more diverse approach which would include more evaluation being done independently. This could be undertaken by specialist consultants, but equally could be done by intermediaries with relevant expertise. There is also a value to self-evaluation, with communities themselves evaluating the outcomes of certain projects. Such an exercise could have clear capacity building benefits, with the results being more likely to be accepted and acted upon. Initially, support could be provided in this process and thought given to an appropriate process and criteria.

Disseminating the results

Evaluation is closely tied to dissemination. Information and guidance about what works and what doesn't is a logical consequence of the evaluative process. Unfortunately, in practice, this information is not used to best effect. There needs to be a requirement on agencies leading area regeneration programmes to produce information which can be used on a national, regional and even local basis. It needs collating regionally and nationally. It should be available regularly and frequently for it to have maximum benefit. It needs to be disseminated in a number of forms, on paper, through IT systems and in seminars. And it should be widely disseminated, not just to agencies but also to communities and the voluntary sector.

This more frequent and up-to-date dissemination of information would complement the more thorough evaluations commissioned, such as those by government, of area regeneration programmes nationally.

A strategic approach to intermediaries

Intermediary organisations are a key feature in the resourcing of community involvement – much of what they do is capacity building. They can directly support groups involved in area regeneration programmes; as independent organisations they can play a vital role in mediating between communities and professional agencies – especially local authorities – when necessary, and can employ community development workers, and support those employed by other agencies. In particular, they are essential in supporting small mutual aid and self-help groups which have informal structures and often have no formal relationship with local or central government (Burns and Taylor, 1998).

An incomplete network

However, there are problems. The geographical spread of intermediary organisations is patchy. Many of the most deprived communities do not have access to them and where they do exist, their quality is variable. Some offer very high quality services and support mechanisms; others are less effective. Many are financially insecure, depending to varying extents upon payments of fees for services from community groups which themselves are poorly funded and, in particular, have difficulty in accessing funding to buy support services. Most have to 'follow the money', resulting in the development of projects and programmes which may not be in accord with the needs of local communities.

A significant number of intermediaries have yet to catch up with the requirements of communities involved in regeneration programmes. An increasingly complex policy environment necessitates the development of new skills and a strategic approach. In this respect and others, intermediaries often need capacity building themselves in order to develop the expertise of staff and management.

Few intermediaries are wholly independent. Many are local authority funded, which can compromise the relationship they have with community groups as they cannot always afford to come into conflict with the authority on the side of residents. Some, particularly those that are subsidiaries of larger service organisations, have agendas which may bring them into direct conflict with their parent bodies.

Filling the intermediary gaps

Fundamentally, there is no overall strategic approach towards the spread, funding or quality of intermediary organisations. Several things need to happen to put this in place. Firstly, central government needs to take responsibility for supporting the nationally-based umbrella organisations. Secondly, the Regional Development Agencies should be encouraged to develop regional strategies aimed at promoting an infrastructure of intermediaries of a type appropriate and accessible to the needs of local communities. This will require an audit of what exists in each region, an evaluation of quality and a clear analysis of need on the part of local communities. Thirdly, intermediaries themselves must develop their own relationships with government agencies, particularly through their involvement in the national strategy for neighbourhood renewal.

Building the strength of local intermediaries

Finsbury Park Community Trust, North London

Finsbury Park Community Trust was created in 1986 by local people who decided that successful community action required a strong community-based intermediary organisation to deliver successful local projects. Although its geographical area of operation now extends across inner North London, the Trust still draws the majority of its membership from the communities in Finsbury Park, with local people currently holding four of the 13 places on the Board. It is a successful local intermediary specialising in community-based economic and social regeneration.

One of the Trust's primary roles is to support other local community groups through the provision of techncial advice and assistance. It spends 14% (£130,000) of its annual budget on community capacity building work, currently supporting four programmes, carried out in partnership with other agencies.

One of these programmes, known as 'Tottenham Pathways', runs in parallel with 13 similar projects in London and is supported by SRB and European Social Fund Objective 3, Priority 4 funding. It supports the development of small, local community groups in three ways:

- by offering training to local people to become outreach workers for the voluntary and community sector;

- by producing a planning guide for 10 community groups and providing seminars to help them develop their capacity;

- by operating a one-stop shop advice service on one of the local estates which offers a 'bridge' for local people to move from their own locality into the world of employment and training.

The Trust is a key partner in a London-wide consortium of organisations using another tranche of European Social Fund money to deliver capacity building services to black and minority ethnic organisations, primarily to stimulate community businesses and tackle unemployment. Its 'Missing Links' programme, focused on training and employment initiatives and funded through SRB4, includes a small capacity building project for the four community-based organisations involved in the partnership.

As part of its work as a local capacity builder, the Trust is also supporting, at its own expense, the development of another, unfunded local community organisation – The Triangle Community Trust. It also operates a small grants programme for voluntary and community groups in Finsbury Park which runs at around £70,000 a year.

The Trust is a good example of how local communities can develop their own local solutions to key problems and attract significant funding to underpin a broad range of community-based initiatives which might otherwise have struggled for support and advice.

7

A financial approach to filling the gaps

There are never enough financial resources for urban regeneration initiatives. Regeneration is a cyclical process, moving from one area to another as social and economic circumstances change. Often these changes can be fast and dramatic, generating a plethora of initiatives to tackle familiar problems. Key agencies not infrequently find themselves returning time and time again to the same communities and neighbourhoods, without ever quite managing to stabilise them and deliver genuinely sustainable futures. It is certainly not for want of trying.

While it must be right to concentrate scarce regeneration resources on neighbourhoods which suffer the most from social exclusion and deprivation, the inevitable result is that while some communities are prioritised, others are left behind. The emphasis on competitive bidding, with its winners and losers, has tended to exclude a significant number of urban communities which arguably are equally in need of help. There are many small pockets of deprivation in non-priority urban areas and urban villages in predominantly rural areas which find it hard to access any significant resources to build the capacity of their communities, let alone regenerate their neighbourhoods.

Funding capacity building – a national target

Whatever the resource distribution process, building community capacity in urban neighbourhoods is a vital process which must be properly funded. A 10-year effort to tackle the 3,000 deprived neighbourhoods within the *Bringing Britain together* strategy for neighbourhood renewal would mean setting a target of 300 neighbourhoods each year. Existing resources for capacity building will inevitably be thinly spread.

There is much debate, and little research, about what constitutes a desirable level of community activity in any given neighbourhood. A minimum benchmark figure of £30,000 a year might enable each neighbourhood to employ a community development worker, buy in training and support services from an intermediary, and run a programme of activities to build up their social capital and their capacity to engage effectively in their regeneration programmes. Around £9 million would be needed in the first year to support a rather basic, national programme along these lines.

Neighbourhoods waiting their turn in the programme would benefit from pump-priming funding, to help them establish their social capital prior to their inclusion in the full programme. An allocation of £5,000 per neighbourhood would add £13.5 million to the budgetary requirement in the first year.

Although no one has calculated how much is actually invested in community capacity building within the 3,000 neighbourhoods each year, we can be reasonably confident that it is well below this minimum figure. The primary assets in any regeneration area are the people who live there. Investment in them is the key to long-term sustainability. So what needs to be done? What changes in financial resourcing would help to make a significant impact on the ability of communities to fully involve themselves in regenerating their neighbourhoods?

What needs to be done?

Finding new money

- Top slicing existing area regeneration programme budgets and lottery grants to enable communities to buy in advice, support and training from local intermediaries.
- Establishing a Neighbourhood Empowerment Fund to substantially boost the resources available, and specifically target embryonic community groups unable to access mainstream funding.
- Match funding the Neighbourhood Empowerment Fund with finance from other providers *before they are applied for*, along the lines being piloted by the South Yorkshire Key Fund.
- Drawing in more support from the private sector, particularly through endowments and social lending by major companies and financial institutions.

Strategic targeting

- Targeting communities and regions where community involvement is low level and local intermediaries are either weak or thinly spread.
- Helping communities on the margins compete for regeneration resources.

- Introducing sanctions for regeneration agencies which secure funding, but do not subsequently deliver on community involvement. This requires effective evaluation methods, which are not yet in place and must avoid penalising local communities themselves.
- Prioritising government support for voluntary and community-led regeneration bids, through the SRB and New Deal for Communities programmes.
- Targeting existing non-government funding programmes, particularly the lottery programmes, on the 3,000 most deprived neighbourhoods.
- Investing in long-term, rather than short-term programmes of capacity building, throughout the life of area regeneration initiatives.

Funding diversity

- Avoiding standardised funding packages which constrain rather than enable the community capacity building process.
- Providing flexibility in funding programmes, enabling and encouraging a variety of solutions to issues and problems identified by communities themselves.
- Generating wider acceptance among funders that investment in community capacity building involves risk and that normal

---

Making matched funding work for communities

South Yorkshire Key Fund

The Development Trusts Association is part of a local consortium that has successfully bid to manage a new and innovative European fund being piloted in South Yorkshire. The Key Fund is a response from the European Union to the frequent complaints from community-based organisations about the difficulties of accessing and managing European funding. The Fund will be used to provide technical assistance and support to community organisations involved in sustainable employment, regeneration initiatives and grass-roots approaches to active citizenship.

£1.7 million is being made available over two years, with technical support available for three years. Individual grants of up to £25,000 are available and community groups have access to both a call centre and one-stop shop for both initial and ongoing support and advice.

All the funds are being pre-matched by the four local authorities and three TECs in South Yorkshire, thus removing one of the key barriers to European funding for community organisations. The Fund also has a very simple application process – including a two-page application form – and is paid out according to project need, in advance rather than in arrears. Evaluation of the project is underway and, if successful, the Development Trusts Association will be seeking to replicate it across the UK.

funding criteria, such as output measures, efficiency and value for money are less important than outcomes and effectiveness.

Reducing the administrative burden

- Ensuring that a higher proportion of the available resources for community capacity building finds its way down to grass-roots level.
- Streamlining the delivery process, by fast-tracking community applications for capacity building funds, along the lines of the National Lottery Charities Board's Awards for All scheme.
- Using innovative techniques, such as call centres and one-stop shops, to improve accessibility for applicants and reduce management costs.

Creating a client culture

- Channelling capacity building funds, wherever possible, direct to local communities themselves, so they can buy in the support they need from local intermediaries.

Regional decision making

- Giving RDAs a role in delivering central government funding for capacity building to community groups and intermediaries in their areas, while focusing central government support for capacity building on grant aid for national umbrella and representative bodies.

Coordinated initiatives

- Exploring the potential for joint programmes, where several funders are involved in support for a range of similar community initiatives in the same neighbourhood or region.

Building community assets

- Accepting that the community ownership of resources and assets can contribute significantly to area regeneration.
- Prioritising support funding of community controlled vehicles, such as development trusts and foundations, which can provide long-term sustainability through asset transfer or new provision.

Funding a comprehensive network of locally-based intermediaries

- Providing core funding, possibly through RDAs, to fill the gaps and help establish an effective regional network of local intermediaries to provide capacity building support.
- Supporting a range of different intermediaries, with no preferred model.
- Focusing on building the strength of appropriate existing agencies before setting up new ones. For example by:
  - supporting interested housing associations to become community investment agencies in some areas, making use of their asset base and access to potential new resources through The Housing Corporation for community capacity building;
  - encouraging established development trusts to broaden their brief and geographical coverage;
  - developing a strategic network of community foundations, possibly by piloting a network in one region, with RDA funding;
  - promoting a wider regional network of Community Chests;
  - developing the emerging voluntary sector regional networks to support local intermediaries.

Evaluating the investment

- Establishing baseline information on community involvement in regeneration areas.
- Agreeing an effective method of evaluating the investment in community capacity building across all funding programmes.
- Subsequently, introducing new criteria and measures to put the agreed evaluation method into practice.
- Allocating DETR funding to pilot the agreed evaluation method.

8

A Neighbourhood Empowerment Fund

Background

Outline proposals for establishing a national community resource fund were first floated by the Joseph Rowntree Foundation in 1995 (Taylor, 1995). At that time, it was suggested that such a Fund could offer:

- Targeted start-up support to local organisations wishing to develop strategic visions or action plans for their neighbourhoods, with a view to securing regeneration funds to tackle local problems.
- Small-scale funds for residents' activities which fall outside the scope of other funding initiatives.
- Initial training, confidence building and leadership development – essential elements in the development of strong local organisations and active citizenry.

It was felt that a fund of perhaps £10 million annually could either be supported by public sector grant, or through lottery programmes, with the possibility of a contribution from the private sector.

These outline ideas have recently been under active consideration by the government's Social Exclusion Unit, specifically by Policy Action Team 9 (Community Self-Help) (SEU, 1999). It recommended to Ministers that a fund offering grants of between £50 and £500 to community organisations be established under the auspices of the Home Office's Active Community Unit. An announcement backing these proposals was made by Home Office minister, Paul Boateng, in September 1999 (Home Office Press Release, 16 September 1999).

Valuable as such a fund will undoubtedly be to many existing community organisations, its limited scope and lack of neighbourhood focus would do little to tackle the significant resource gaps identified in this report. A larger, more strategic vehicle is clearly needed which focuses directly on urban neighbourhoods, ties in closely with the national strategy for neighbourhood renewal and funds activities which empower local communities involved in regeneration programmes.

In short, there is a need for a substantial Neighbourhood Empowerment Fund.

The views of key stakeholders

The success of any new fund depends, in part, on securing support for it from those most active in the field of community capacity building and regeneration. As a key part of the research for this report, we were therefore keen to establish views and opinions about a Neighbourhood Empowerment Fund from a broad range of national and local organisations with a direct interest in how it should be established. A list of those consulted is included in the Appendix.

There was widespread agreement that a Neighbourhood Empowerment Fund would be a welcome addition to the financial mechanisms available to local communities. There was also a significant measure of agreement about what the main features of any new fund should be. These included the following 10 key points:

1. Regional decision making.
2. Targeting funding on community groups themselves and on areas excluded from mainstream regeneration funding.
3. Easy accessibility for groups.
4. Flexible funding packages which recognise local diversity.
5. Long-term support for groups rather than short-term programmes.
6. Pre-matched funding from public and private sector sources.
7. Avoidance of duplication of existing funding regimes.
8. Voluntary and community sector involvement in delivery.
9. Minimisation of administrative costs.
10. Effective evaluation of the fund's impact on capacity building.

There was predictably less agreement about who should establish and administer the fund, although there was a general view that central and local government should play a supportive rather than a lead role. There was also some uncertainty about whether a fund of £10 million annually was large enough to make a strategic impact on the problem.

We have taken these views into account in framing the following proposals for the Neighbourhood Empowerment Fund.

Outline for a Neighbourhood Empowerment Fund

Fund size

A national fund for England of £10 million per annum should be piloted from 2001 for three years, with the intention to increase funding incrementally to £20 million by the end of this period and then held at this level, subject to inflation increases, for a further seven years.

Funding sources

Initial funding should come from the following sources:

National Lottery Charities Board 50%
Top slicing SRB Challenge Fund 50%

Within two years of start-up, we would expect to see the funding base extended to include European funding and support from the private sector, primarily through endowments. By year three, therefore, the funding sources could be as follows:

National Lottery Charities Board 35%
Top slicing SRB Challenge Fund 35%
European programmes 20%
Private sector endowments 10%

Key objectives

The primary objectives of the Fund should be:

- To enable local communities to articulate their own priorities for urban regeneration, at the earliest possible stage in the process.
- To help build the social capital of deprived urban neighbourhoods, through support for a range of small-scale community initiatives.

Targeting

The Fund should be targeted initially on the following priorities:

- small-scale, pump-priming activities in disadvantaged communities with little or no access to mainstream regeneration funding;
- communities bidding for regeneration funds, either in their own right, or as lead agents in partnerships, to assist in the preparation of community plans;
- limited-life core funding to fill the gaps and help establish an effective national network of local intermediaries to provide capacity building support;
- regions underperforming on community involvement in area regeneration programmes.

Administration

How the Fund is set up and administered is of vital importance. Any proposals to locate the Fund within the Active Community Unit of the Home Office are unlikely to be well received by the voluntary and community sector. We support the view that the Neighbourhood Empowerment Fund should be, and be seen to be, a voluntary and community sector-led initiative. This is an important opportunity to build the capacity of the sector nationally and develop more cohesion between its constituent parts. This rules out placing it within a government department – particularly one which is not expected to have a financial interest in its performance.

Alternative proposals to place the Fund under the umbrella of the National Lottery Charities Board have more merit, not least because the Board has experience in community resourcing, a regional decision-making framework and a small grants fund (Awards for All) which has some parallels with the Neighbourhood Empowerment Fund. We expect the Board to be a key funder and will therefore have an important stake in the outcome.

However, our view is that the role of the National Lottery Charities Board should be more limited, focusing on the setting-up arrangements, providing ongoing administrative support to minimise additional core costs, and acting as advisors to the Fund operators.

We have given consideration to whether the operation of the Fund should be tendered, inviting responses from the private sector. While this might deliver benefits in terms of lower running costs and value for money, private sector operation would lack community credibility and is probably not appropriate for a fund of this nature. Nevertheless, it should be held in reserve as an option beyond the three-year initial pilot period.

Our preferred option is to establish a consortium of national voluntary and community sector bodies which would take overall responsibility for the operation of the fund. Although the final composition of the consortium and its leadership would be a matter for early discussion within the sector, we would expect some or all of the following national bodies to be involved:

National Council for Voluntary Organisations
Urban Forum
National Federation of Community Organisations (Community Matters)
National Association of Councils for Voluntary Service
Development Trusts Association
Association of Community Trusts and Foundations
British Association of Settlements and Social Action Centres
Standing Conference on Community Development
Black Training and Enterprise Group
Confederation of Indian Organisations

It would also be appropriate to involve the Community Development Foundation in this group. All these organisations have differing agendas and none have a specific focus on neighbourhood regeneration. It will therefore be vital to ensure that there is a very clear national remit from government for the Neighbourhood Empowerment Fund, to ensure that there is no 'leakage' into other activities.

The consortium would need to have a close working relationship with a sponsoring government department, to ensure accountability and probity. The DETR is strategically best placed to perform this role and we would recommend that this is agreed by government at an early stage.

Implementation

The Fund operators would have a national strategic role, be accountable to funders and government, and make decisions on regional allocations. It is vital that all grant decisions are made as locally as possible, but establishing regional offices is clearly not appropriate for a fund of this size and would be unnecessarily bureaucratic. Our conclusions point to a franchise arrangement, with regionally based intermediaries, either alone or in partnership, tendering to operate the devolved funds. This would allow for regional variation in the location, quality and expertise of intermediaries.

The regional funds should operate along the lines being piloted in South Yorkshire through the Key Fund, with:

- pre-matched funding;
- a simple, short application procedure (two pages maximum);
- a call centre and help-line for applicants;
- ongoing support and advice;
- funding in advance, rather than in arrears.

We are also aware of proposals from Policy Action Team 9 and Community Matters for the establishment of community technical assistance vouchers. These would enable community groups to access advice and support without the need for the administrative and financial accounting requirements associated with grants. In our view, this approach is worth piloting alongside the Neighbourhood Empowerment Fund, perhaps in two regions, to test the validity of the assumptions behind it.

Evaluation

The Neighbourhood Empowerment Fund should be formally evaluated by DETR at the end of its three-year pilot period.

Conclusions

The emerging *Bringing Britain together* strategy for neighbourhood renewal rightly places great importance on the central role local communities can and must play in securing a better quality of life for themselves. These communities are, for the first time, being offered the chance to shape their neighbourhoods and take a lead role in the process of change. But, in all but a few cases, this won't happen by itself, nor will it happen overnight. To happen at all the process must be properly resourced:

- it needs the right type of support, from central government down to individual community development workers;
- it needs coordinated action, at national, regional and local level;
- it needs new, inclusive and holistic forms of local management;
- it needs significant shifts in institutional cultures;
- it needs targeted funding.

Establishing a Neighbourhood Empowerment Fund is important, but it is only one piece of the jigsaw. Neighbourhood regeneration is a challenging agenda and one which must succeed. This report helps to point the way forward.

References

Barr, A., Hashagen, S. and Purcell, R. (1996) *Monitoring and evaluation of community development in Northern Ireland*, Belfast: Voluntary Activity Unit, Department of Health and Social Services.

Burns, D. and Taylor, M. (1998) *Mutual aid and self-help: Coping strategies for excluded communities*, Bristol: The Policy Press.

Burrows, R. and Rhodes, D. (1998) *Unpopular places?: Area disadvantage and the geography of misery in England*, Bristol: The Policy Press.

Chanan, G., West, A., Garratt, C. and Humm, J. (1999) *Regeneration and sustainable communities*, London: Community Development Foundation.

DETR (Department of the Environment, Transport and the Regions) (1998a) *1998 Index of Deprivation: A summary of results*, London: DETR.

DETR (1998b) *Single Regeneration Budget bidding guidance: A guide for partnerships*, London: DETR.

DETR (1998c) *Modernising local government: Improving local services through Best Value*, London: DETR.

DETR (1999) *New Deal for Communities: Developing delivery plans*, London: DETR.

Dwelly, T. (1999) *Community investment: The growing role for housing associations*, York: JRF.

Filkin, G., Bassam, Lord, Corrigan, P., Stoker, G. and Tizard, J. (1999) *Starting to modernise*, York: JRF.

Hall, S. and Mawson, J. (1999) *Challenge funding, contracts and area regeneration: A decade of innovation in policy management and co-ordination*, Bristol: The Policy Press.

JRF (Joseph Rowntree Foundation) (1998) *Regenerating neighbourhoods: Creating integrated and sustainable improvements*, York: JRF.

JRF (1999) *Developing effective community involvement strategies: Guidance for Single Regeneration Budget bids*, York: JRF.

Knight, B., Suerdon, M. and Pharoah, C. (eds) (1998) *Building a civil society*, London: Charities Aid Foundation.

SEU (Social Exclusion Unit) (1998) *Bringing Britain together: A national strategy for neighbourhood renewal*, London: Home Office.

SEU (1999) *Report of the Policy Action Team on community self-help*, London: Active Community Unit, Home Office.

Skinner, S. (1997) *Building community strengths: A resource book on capacity building*, London: Community Development Foundation.

Taylor, M. (1995) *Bringing residents to the centre of regeneration*, York: JRF.

Taylor, M. (2000) *Top down meets bottom up: Neighbourhood management*, York: JRF.

Appendix: Organisations contributing to the study

The following national and regional organisations and individuals were consulted as part of this study.

Gaynor Humphries	Association of Community Trusts and Foundations
Martin Booth	Banks of the Wear Limited
Anne Murray	Baring Foundation
Sajid Butt	Black Training and Enterprise Group
Alison West	Community Development Foundation
Charles Woodd	Community Matters
Rajesh Kalhan	Confederation of Indian Organisations (UK)
John Roberts	DETR, Regeneration Division
John Cross	DETR, Regional Policy Unit
Mary Doyle	Development Trusts Association
Stephen Downs	Government Office North East
Janet Novak	Home Office Active Community Unit
Helen Goody	Local Government Association
Alastair Jackson	National Housing Federation
Stephen Dunmore	National Lottery New Opportunities Fund
Vandna Gohill Sharon Scott	National Lottery Charities Board
Anne Blackmore Richard Grice	National Council for Voluntary Organisations
Peter Counsell	NHS Executive (Northern and Yorkshire)
Fiona Ellis	Northern Rock Foundation
Liz Walton	Social Exclusion Unit, Cabinet Office
Holly Donagh	The Arts Council of England
Adrian Moran	The Housing Corporation
John Routledge	Urban Forum

The following area regeneration projects and individuals participated in the questionnaire survey.

A.F. Pollard	Ashfield Partnership, Nottinghamshire
M. Pearce	Brighton and Hove Council URBAN Initiative
Andrea Tara-Chand	Chapeltown and Harehills Urban Initiative, Leeds
Lynda Hunter	Chesterfield Area Regeneration Team
A. Modu	Finsbury Park Community Trust
Resham Aujla	Greater Nottingham Partnership
Pat Mundy	Hartcliffe and Withywood Ventures, Bristol
Graham Williams	Hendon SRB, Sunderland
Sade Johnson	Holly Street Comprehensive Estates Initiative, Hackney, London
Kirsty Duncanson	Mansfield Diamond Partnership
Helena Kettleborough	Middleton Pride, Lancashire
Ian McKinnon	North Tyneside City Challenge
Sylvia Burn	North Hartlepool Partnership
Marilyn Taylor	O-Regen, Waltham Forest, London
Catherine McManus	Progress Trust, Manchester
Barbara Coleman	Regeneration in West Chester
David Garbutt	SESKU, Wakefield, Yorkshire
Nicola Wade	Skillswork, Woolwich. London
Kevin Stower	Thanet Council Community Regeneration Unit, Kent
Damien Telford Wilson	Tidworth SRB, Kennet
Peter Aviston	Walsall SRB Partnership
Ian Hill	West Cumbria CVS
Kevin Ward/Tony Herrmann	West Yorkshire Community Work Training Group/University of Leeds

Learning Resources
Centre